MW00913032

AMERICAN HISTORY BY DECADE

The

1980s

Titles in the American History by Decade series are:

The 1900s
The 1910s
The 1920s
The 1930s
The 1940s
The 1950s
The 1960s
The 1970s
The 1980s
The 1990s

AMERICAN HISTORY BY DECADE

The
1980s

Kris Hirschmann

KIDHAVEN PRESS™

THOMSON
━━━━━━✦━━━━━━™
GALE

San Diego • Detroit • New York • San Francisco • Cleveland
New Haven, Conn. • Waterville, Maine • London • Munich

LIBRARY OF CONGRESS CATALOGING-IN-PUBLICATION DATA

Hirschmann, Kris, 1967–
  The 1980s / by Kris Hirschmann.
    p. cm. — (American History by Decade)
Summary: Discusses the 1980s including the Cold War, personal computers, AIDS,
and music videos.
Includes bibliographical references and index.
  ISBN 0-7377-1750-5 (hardback : alk. paper)
1. United States—History—1980—Juvenile literature. 2. Nineteen eighties—
Juvenile literature. [1. United States—History—1980– 2. Nineteen eighties.]
I. Title: Nineteen eighties. II. Title. III. Series.
  E876.H57 2004
  973.927--dc21

                                                                    2003009949

Contents

A Time of Change

The one word that seems to sum up the 1980s is "change." The decade saw extreme changes in politics, technology, health care, and entertainment. These changes had lasting effects on American industries and lifestyles.

The political changes of the 1980s were driven by new feelings of national pride. "The era of self-doubt is over," said U.S. president Ronald Reagan early in the decade. Reagan was referring to the 1970s, when America's confidence was low. The country had lost a long war in Vietnam, President Nixon had quit in disgrace, and the economy was falling apart. But Reagan was determined to change the national attitude. "We have every right to dream heroic dreams,"[1] he said.

One of Reagan's "heroic dreams" was to make America the most powerful country in the world. With the support of the American people, Reagan poured money into the U.S. military. His actions eventually turned America into the world's strongest **superpower**.

America's technological revolution was another source of pride. Personal computers in particular caused huge changes in **productivity** and lifestyles. Computer technology seemed almost magical, and it made Americans feel that anything was possible.

Cable television technology did not seem as magical as computers. But this 1980s invention, too, changed the way Americans live. People went from getting just a few publicly broadcast television stations to receiving dozens of special-interest channels via a cable connection. One of these channels, MTV, showed nothing but music videos. The channel's creators hoped simply to attract an audience. Instead, they started a revolution that forever changed the way people enjoy music.

The **AIDS epidemic**, which began in 1981 and got worse throughout the decade, was a negative blot on a mostly positive period. The world's best scientists were unable to cure or even slow the deadly disease. By the end of the decade, the fear of AIDS had changed the way people live. This change and others helped define and shape the decade of the 1980s.

Then and Now

	1980	2000
U.S. population:	226,546,000	281,421,906
Life expectancy:	Female: 77.6 Male: 69.9	Female: 79.5 Male: 74.1
Average yearly salary:	$15,757	$35,305
Minimum wage:	$3.10 per hour	$5.15 per hour

Sources: Bureau of Labor Statistics; Kingwood College Library; *National Vital Statistics Reports*, vol. 51, no. 3; U.S. Census Bureau.

CHAPTER ONE

The Cold War Ends

One of the most important events of the 1980s was the end of the Cold War. The Cold War was a long-running conflict between the United States and the Soviet Union (known today as the Russian Federation). It was not a traditional war. The military forces of the United States and the Soviet Union did not fight each other on a battlefield or launch missiles against each other. Instead, the Cold War was a struggle for power and influence.

The Cold War created constant tension between the United States and the Soviet Union. This tension trickled down to other nations around the world. Countries picked sides and threatened each other. Traditional warfare, with battles and soldiers and death, seemed like it could break out at any moment.

At the beginning of the 1980s the Cold War was in full swing. By the end of the decade, however, the conflict was over. The events that led to the end of the Cold War defined world politics during the 1980s.

Cold War Background

The Cold War began after World War II ended in 1945. The United States and the Soviet Union had been allies during the war. After the war both countries agreed to help rebuild and manage war-torn parts of Europe. However, they had very different ideas about how this should be done. Both nations tried to enforce their own ideas. As a result, distrust grew quickly between the United States and the Soviet Union.

Because of this distrust, the two nations began developing powerful weapons. Neither country intended to attack the other. The weapons were insurance in case the other nation struck. Before long, however, the buildup got out of

THE SOVIET UNION AND THE RUSSIAN FEDERATION

The Soviet Union, seen here in red and brown, collapsed in 1991 and separated into fifteen separate countries. The area in red is known today as the Russian Federation.

MOLDOVA

LITHUANIA
LATVIA

ESTONIA

BELARUS

UKRAINE

AZERBAIJAN

KAZAKHSTAN

GEORGIA
ARMENIA

TURKMENISTAN

UZBEKISTAN

KYRGYZSTAN

TAJIKISTAN

RUSSIA

North Sea
Norwegian Sea
White Sea
Kara Sea
Bering Sea
Sea of Okhotsk
Black Sea
Caspian Sea
Aral Sea
Lake Balkhash
Lake Baikal
Persian Gulf
Sea of Japan
Yellow Sea

Detail Area

U.S. soldiers work on a missile launch vehicle. The United States created many powerful weapons during the arms race.

control. Each time one country developed a new weapon, the other rushed to create an even bigger and deadlier one. This situation was known as the **arms race**. Over time, both the United States and the Soviet Union created many powerful weapons. Some of these, such as nuclear missiles, had so much force that they could wipe major cities off the face of the earth. Each country used its weapons to scare the other country and keep it from attacking.

At the same time, the United States and the Soviet Union worked to gain influence in smaller nations around the world. By doing this, each country hoped to make its circle of "friends" bigger. In the Cold War world, more friends meant more power and therefore more security.

The Early 1980s

By the early 1980s a deep divide existed between the United States and the Soviet Union. Many Americans believed all Soviets were bad people who might turn violent without warning. They also feared **communism**, the idea behind the Soviet form of government. In a true Communist society, all people are equal in every way. This sounds good in theory, but the reality was not so pleasant. Soviet leadership had to keep strict control over every part of its citizens' lives to enforce its rules. Many of the things that happened in the Soviet Union and other Communist nations seemed harsh and frightening to Americans.

In this atmosphere, Ronald Reagan was elected president of the United States. Reagan was elected partly because he had promised to lead America in a worldwide fight against communism. After Reagan took office in January 1981 he immediately began working to keep his promise. He spent billions of dollars on new weapons. One of these was an antimissile system that would orbit the earth. Reagan said it would be able to destroy any weapons the Soviets might shoot at the United States. This system was officially called the Strategic Defense Initiative, but it was soon nick-named Star Wars.

Star Wars and Reagan's other military programs allowed America to gain the advantage in the arms race. This upset then Soviet leader

Soon after taking office, President Ronald Reagan spent billions of dollars on new weapons.

Yuri Andropov, who worried that America's new weapons were a threat to world peace. He complained about Reagan's policies, saying, "Engaging in this [buildup] is not just irresponsible. It is insane."[2] Reagan shot back, calling the Soviet Union an "evil empire" and "the focus of evil in the modern world."[3] Tensions soared, and war seemed to loom.

A technician conducts research on weapons for the Strategic Defense Initiative.

Economic Troubles

The Soviet Union was putting up a brave front with its public comments. But in truth, the nation could not afford to keep up with the American arms buildup. Years of massive defense spending and unwise use of natural resources had hurt the Soviet economy. Also, government control had crippled the nation's businesses. For these reasons and others, the economy of the Soviet Union was near collapse by the mid-1980s. Citizens in cities had trouble getting even the most basic foods, such as bread and milk. When these items were available, people had to stand in long lines just to buy their share.

In 1985 a politician named Mikhail Gorbachev was appointed to lead the Soviet Union. Gorbachev knew that his nation did not have the money to keep building weapons. The day after he took charge, Gorbachev made a speech to the world. "We want to stop and not to continue the arms race,"[4] he said.

Reagan responded immediately, saying, "We're ready to work with the Soviet Union for more constructive relations."[5] For the first time in decades, there was hope that the Cold War might ease.

Changing Attitudes

Gorbachev made other important changes. One of the biggest changes involved the Soviet presence in Eastern Europe. Since World War II, the Soviet Union had controlled the governments of many Eastern European countries. In 1988, however, Gorbachev announced his plans to withdraw Soviet troops from Europe. These European countries would now be free to choose their own leaders.

Almost immediately, governments across Eastern Europe began to fall. One by one, countries set up new governments. The United States and other nations watched to see

German citizens climb over the Berlin Wall in November 1989. The wall separated East Berlin and West Berlin for twenty-eight years.

if Gorbachev would keep his promise to stay out of things. He did.

The biggest test of Gorbachev's resolve came in November 1989, when crowds of German citizens tore down the Berlin Wall. This wall had been built in 1961. It separated West Berlin (the American-influenced half of the city of Berlin) from East Berlin (the Soviet-influenced half). The Berlin Wall was a symbol of the Soviet presence in Europe. By allowing this wall to be torn down, Gorbachev showed the world that he was committed to the ideas he preached.

Decade's End

With the end of the arms race and the fall of communism in Eastern Europe, the Cold War was basically over. People began to feel more secure as the threat of nuclear war faded. The United States and the Soviet Union still distrusted each other, but the intense distrust of earlier years was dying down. As the 1980s drew to a close, it appeared that the seeds of lasting peace had been sown.

CHAPTER TWO

The Computer Revolution

In the 1980s an exciting new technology swept America and the world. This new technology was the personal computer (PC).

Personal computers were like nothing the public had ever seen before. They were small enough to fit on a desk. They were cheap enough to be affordable for the average American. And they were powerful enough to run **word processing** programs, **spreadsheets**, games, and other **software**. People loved them. In 1980 more than seven hundred thousand PCs were sold. That was just the beginning. Sales doubled in 1981 to 1.4 million and nearly doubled again in 1982 to 2.4 million. Each succeeding year saw an increase in sales. By the end of the decade, PCs would be in many millions of homes and offices all over the world.

What Computers Were Like

The earliest personal computers may have been powerful by the standards of the time, but they were very primitive compared to the equipment of today. For example, the first PCs did not have hard drives. Every program and file had to be recorded onto **floppy disks** instead of inside the computer. Floppy disks were flexible storage cards that slid into slots on the computer's front panel. Users changed floppy disks frequently while they were working to get all the information they needed.

Early PCs were also very slow compared to today's computers. It might take a PC several minutes to open up a program, save a file, or do other simple tasks. Using a computer involved a lot of waiting.

Bill Gates, head of Microsoft, flings a floppy disk into the air. Early computers used such disks to store information.

In addition to their memory and speed problems, early computers could also be confusing. The first thing a person saw after turning on a PC was a dark screen with a few letters and an arrow in the upper left-hand corner. Commands had to be typed after the arrow to make the computer do anything. Users had to memorize dozens of commands to make their computers work.

Using computers became easier as technology improved. By the mid-1980s users no longer had to memorize com-

Early computers required users to type lines of commands on a dark screen.

mands. They could perform many tasks by pointing at and clicking on things with an on-screen arrow. The arrow was controlled by a handheld device called a mouse. This system was simple and easy to understand. At this point, many people who had complained that computers were confusing finally gave in and bought their first PC.

Computers at Home

Personal computers were a huge hit for one main reason: They made everyday tasks much easier. At home, people found dozens of uses for these wonder machines. One of the most important uses is word processing. People were amazed to discover how simple it was to type text into a word processing program, format it, and print it out. It was much easier than using a typewriter, which gives users no simple way to correct mistakes. Soon word processors were being used for homework, letters, and anything else that involves writing.

Spreadsheets were also popular. Spreadsheets were programs that let people keep track of their money, bills, and other records. Computers did not make mathematical errors, so computer record-keeping was a big improvement over old methods. Also, information could easily be added to or removed from a spreadsheet as situations changed. For instance, a forgotten check could be entered in its proper place long after the date it was written. Tasks like this were hard under manual record-keeping systems, but spreadsheets made them quick and easy.

Home computers were not just used for serious tasks, of course. They were also used for fun. Arcade games like Pong, Space Invaders, and Asteroids were made into home computer games. Later in the decade, more complicated games such as Flight Simulator, Tetris, and Pac-Man were released. Computer games eventually became so popular that many people bought personal computers just for this purpose.

Teenagers play a computer game. Many people bought computers just to play games on them.

Computers at Work

If personal computers were useful at home, they were doubly useful at work. Office workers quickly came to depend on computers for help with word processing tasks. Computers also made accounting, billing, inventory, and business planning easier and faster. With the help of a computer, one person could do as much work as several people who did not have PCs.

At first computers were found mostly in law offices and other businesses that did knowledge-based work. But computers were so helpful that they soon spread to every industry. By the end of the 1980s computers were being used in stores, factories, airports, police departments, and churches, to name just a few places. They were running everything from farms to fisheries to construction sites. Personal computers ruled the world of work.

In the 1980s computers became common in businesses like this fruit packing center.

Schools began offering computer courses in the late 1980s to better prepare students for the business world.

Personal computers also began moving into schools. School officials saw the way computers were changing the business world. They believed students would need computer skills if they wanted to be hired for jobs when they graduated. So computer courses became part of many schools' educational programs. Some schools also set up computer labs, where students could use public computers to do their homework. The youth of America were getting ready to take their place in a computerized world.

A New Passion

Between the workplace, home, and school, PCs had an immediate effect on the lives of most Americans. Computers were everywhere, and as time went by, they became harder and harder to avoid.

By the end of the decade, computers were commonplace. Americans used them at home, at work, and in school.

Some people did not want to learn how to use computers. They complained loudly about the new technology and stubbornly refused to buy or use PCs. These negative voices, however, were in the minority. Most people loved computers. As writer Otto Friedrich phrased it in a 1983 article, "The enduring American love affairs with the automobile and the television set are now being transformed into a giddy passion for the personal computer."[6] Sales of PCs and computer-related products shot up throughout the 1980s. By the end of the decade, personal computers were fueling a $70-billion-a-year industry, and there was no sign of a slowdown. The PC had arrived, and there was no turning back.

CHAPTER THREE

AIDS Appears

T hroughout the 1980s a shadow hung over the United
States. This shadow was AIDS. At first striking just a few
victims, the AIDS epidemic grew as the years went by. By the
end of the decade many Americans had died of the disease,
and hundreds of thousands more were infected.

AIDS dominated medical news during the 1980s. As the
information went from bad to worse, people began to fear for
their lives and the lives of their loved ones. This fear—and
the tragedies that caused it—helped to define America in
the 1980s.

AIDS Emerges

The first sign of AIDS appeared in 1981. During this year
alarming reports started coming in to the U.S. Centers for
Disease Control (CDC). This government agency tracks dis-
eases in the United States. The reports said that dozens of
young men in New York and California had suddenly developed rare forms of cancer, pneumonia, and other illnesses.
All of these young men were dying, and no one knew why.

Investigators soon discovered that the young men were
dying because their bodies were not fighting the germs that
cause illness. It was obvious that something was weakening
these men's **immune systems**. Another thing was obvious,

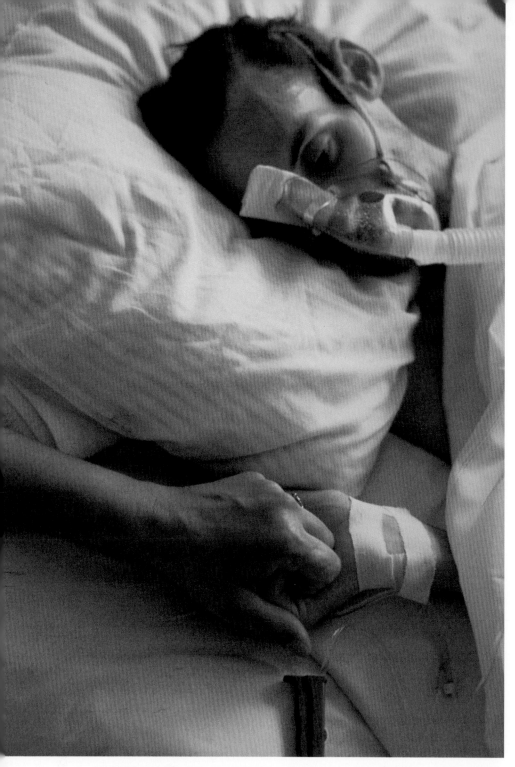

A man suffering from AIDS wears an oxygen mask to help him breathe.

too: The disease was spreading. By the end of 1981 more than three hundred people had come down with the mysterious disease. By the end of the following year, another twelve hundred cases had been reported to the CDC.

Around this time the new disease was given the name AIDS, which stands for Acquired Immunodeficiency Syndrome. No one knew what caused AIDS or how it spread from one person to another. But doctors knew AIDS was deadly. People who developed the disease *always* died.

The Disease Spreads

In the early days AIDS struck only otherwise healthy young men. Most of these young men were homosexuals (people who prefer sexual contact with those of the same sex). People who injected illegal drugs also seemed to be at risk of getting AIDS.

But soon others came down with the disease. One well-known victim was a teenager named Ryan White, who got AIDS from a blood-clotting drug that his doctor had prescribed. White's 1984 case made the public aware that AIDS could spread through blood-based products. Anyone who had received a blood transfusion or received blood products was at risk.

Women also began to get AIDS. One of the earliest female AIDS victims was named Gia Carangi. Carangi was a fashion model who had appeared on the covers of *Vogue*, *Cosmopolitan*, and many other popular magazines. Her death in 1986 proved that women were not safe from AIDS.

The highly publicized cases of Ryan White, Gia Carangi, and others frightened the public. So did the statistics that were being released from the CDC. As 1986 drew to a close, nearly forty-three thousand cases of AIDS had been reported in America. People got more and more worried as the numbers grew.

Teenager Ryan White contracted AIDS from a blood-clotting drug.

Tracking the Killer

By this time scientists knew more about AIDS. In 1983 researchers had discovered that the disease is caused by a **virus**. Viruses cause many types of illness, including the common cold. But the virus that causes AIDS is far from common. Scientists had learned that this virus could remain

In 1983 researchers identified the HIV virus (pictured) as the cause of AIDS.

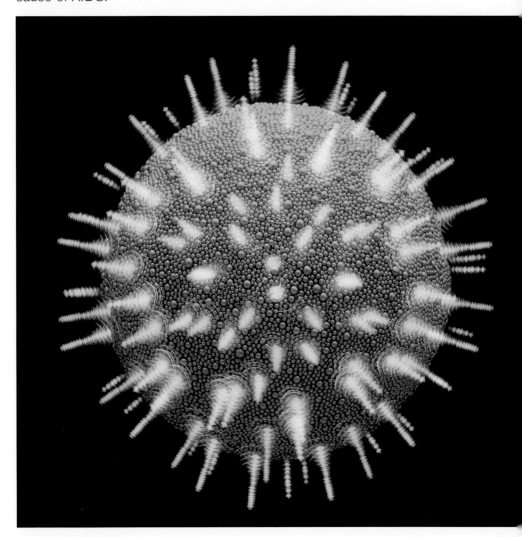

in the body for many years before AIDS developed. This means that seemingly healthy people could carry the disease and unknowingly spread it to others.

Scientists named the AIDS virus **HIV**, which stands for Human Immunodeficiency Virus. They learned that HIV is spread by the exchange of bodily fluids such as blood and semen. The virus is usually spread by sexual contact or by sharing needles for drug injection. It can also be spread by blood transfusions. In addition, infected mothers can pass the virus to their babies either before birth or afterward, through their breast milk.

Knowing these facts did not help scientists cure the disease. Many drugs were developed and tested, but none were successful. A few drugs seemed to slow the disease, but nothing stopped AIDS sufferers from dying.

Public Reaction

Although scientists could not find a cure for AIDS, they did come up with a test that shows whether a person carries HIV. By 1985 this test was available to the public. People could now find out their HIV status.

Many people who thought they were at risk took the test. But others did not. They avoided the test because they did not want their worst fears confirmed. "I wanted to know on the one hand, but then I was afraid to actually confront the reality of an HIV-positive test," explained one person. "I thought, 'What am I going to do if it is positive?' I was not really ready to hear the results."[7]

There was another reason people avoided HIV testing. They did not want to be "branded" by AIDS. In the mid-1980s the public still had a lot of wrong ideas about AIDS. Many people believed that they could be infected if they got near or touched someone with the disease. For this reason, people with HIV and AIDS were often treated poorly. Some

Many people united to create organizations and charities to help those with HIV and AIDS.

AIDS sufferers were fired from their jobs when their condition was discovered. Many others died alone when their frightened friends refused to visit them.

Although fear was the main reaction to AIDS in the mid-1980s, it was not the only one. Many people felt that AIDS sufferers deserved support and kindness instead of fear and hatred. As a result, charities sprang up to help people with AIDS and HIV.

Two people hug at the AIDS Memorial Quilt. The quilt helped to create awareness about HIV and AIDS.

A breakthrough moment for AIDS awareness occurred in 1987, when the AIDS Memorial Quilt was displayed in Washington, D.C. The quilt featured 1,920 handmade panels—one for each person who had died of AIDS up to that point—and it covered an area larger than a football field. This enormous quilt was a stunning and moving comment on the AIDS epidemic. Half a million people visited the quilt in a single weekend. Most came away with a new sympathy for those stricken with AIDS.

Here to Stay

By the end of the 1980s public fear was dying down as people became better educated about the spread of HIV and AIDS. The AIDS epidemic, however, was worse than ever. About 150,000 Americans had already died of the disease, and perhaps a million more were believed to carry the HIV virus. The situation was even worse in other parts of the world. By 1990 the World Health Organization estimated that 8 to 10 million people worldwide were infected with HIV. Of these, about 500,000 were expected to develop AIDS during the coming year.

Driven by these frightening statistics, scientists continued their efforts to develop drugs that could slow or stop AIDS. But nothing looked promising. It was becoming clear that this terrible disease, unknown at the beginning of the decade, was here to stay.

CHAPTER FOUR

Music Videos Change Society

During the 1980s, society was forever changed by a new medium: the music video. Music videos were short movies that went along with songs. These musical clips exploded into the public eye at the beginning of the eighties and steadily grew more and more popular.

As music videos grew in popularity, they became important to a song's success. By the end of the decade, musicians would not dream of releasing a song without making a video to go along with it. Music was no longer something people just listened to. It was something they expected to watch as well.

MTV

Music videos first appeared in the 1970s. However, they did not take off until 1981, when a cable television channel called MTV began broadcasting across America. "MTV" stands for "Music Television." The channel's mission was to show music videos twenty-four hours a day, every day.

In the beginning many of the videos shown on MTV simply showed a band or singer performing a song. But as time went by music videos became more ambitious. Some videos told stories that went along with the song. For example, the group A-Ha did a video for its 1985 song "Take On Me" that showed a girl being sucked into a comic-book world. Inside the comic book, the girl finds danger and romance. At the end of the video, the girl returns to the real world and brings her cartoon boyfriend with her.

Other bands made videos that had nothing to do with the song. Instead, they showed interesting or unusual images that were meant simply to catch the eye. Singer Peter Gabriel's video for the 1985 song "Sledgehammer" used this

Pop group Status Quo performs onstage. Early music videos simply showed bands performing a song.

technique. In this clip, objects such as fruit, dancing chickens, and chalkboards formed an ever-changing, animated version of Gabriel's face.

No matter what music videos contained, they let singers show themselves to their audience in a way that had not been possible before. Videos added a whole new visual dimension to music, and the youth of America loved it. MTV was an instant smash hit.

MTV Addicts

Why did people love music videos so much? Part of the appeal was the thrill of watching singers and bands perform. Before music videos, fans knew musicians mostly from pictures in magazines and on album covers. Sometimes they could see them perform live, but this opportunity came only once in a while. After MTV, however, fans could see how their favorite musicians moved and acted, and they could see it every day. This was new and entertaining.

Viewers also liked the way music videos looked. Directors edited videos to make them choppy, fast moving, and thrilling. Also, musicians often performed against colorful, eye-catching sets. These exciting visuals kept viewers interested and gave them a reason to watch a video even if they did not know the band or singer. And even if a clip was not very interesting, that was OK. Music videos lasted just a few minutes, so viewers usually sat through the boring ones and hoped that something better would come on next.

Music videos quickly became an addiction for young people across America. Kids everywhere stared at MTV for hours as they waited for favorite clips to show up. Often groups of kids even gathered to watch MTV together. At school the next day, they talked about the videos they had seen. Kids who had not seen the videos were left out of the conversation. Music videos therefore were not just something

Singer David Bowie (left) poses on the set of his music video. Music videos with interesting or unusual content were popular.

people watched and enjoyed. They had become part of the social scene, too.

Selling the Music

Viewers were not the only ones who loved music videos. Musicians and record companies adored them as well, because TV exposure meant bigger audiences. Some artists who had been around for years finally became popular when their videos began airing on MTV. Singer Pat Benatar and the band Aerosmith were two acts that had this experience.

Some artists also took advantage of music videos to create unique images. Singer Madonna was especially good at doing this. Madonna's earliest videos showed her wearing miniskirts and torn clothing, lots of dangling jewelry, heavy makeup, and messy hair tied back with lacy handkerchiefs. Madonna's clothing gave viewers the idea that she was fun, exciting, and rebellious. This image helped Madonna to sell records. Why? Fans wanted to be like Madonna. Because they admired the singer, they supported her by buying her music.

Singer Michael Jackson was another artist who used videos to create an image. Jackson's hairstyle, his clothing, and his incredible dancing skills were just a few of the things that defined this singer. Jackson also tried things in his music videos that no one had ever done before. He used dozens of backup dancers, and he experimented with special lighting and makeup effects. He even shot an eleven-minute-long video (a mock 1950s-style horror movie that went with the 1983 song "Thriller"). Viewers were crazy about Jackson's clips, proving that anything was possible in the new world of music videos.

Eighties Style

The popularity of music videos had a big effect on the fashion and styles of the 1980s. People wanted to be like their favorite artists, and the easiest way to do this was by dressing like those artists. The Madonna look was popular with some people. Other people preferred the punk look of singer Billy Idol. These people wore black leather, chains, dog collars, and other outrageous clothing. Still others showed that they were "just regular folks" by dressing in blue jeans and plain white T-shirts like down-to-earth rocker Bruce Springsteen.

Singer Michael Jackson relaxes during filming of the music video, *Billy Jean*.

Madonna's music videos affected the fashions of the 1980s.
Her fans began to dress like she did.

Even people who did not try to copy specific singers were influenced by music videos. "Poofy" hairstyles, colorful and/or torn clothing, and heavy makeup all got their start on MTV. Before long, people who had never watched a music video were wearing leather pants and dying their hair purple.

Music video styles even began to trickle into popular TV shows. The show *Miami Vice*, for instance, featured choppy editing similar to music videos. It also included blaring rock and pop music and a couple of supercool cops who always dressed stylishly and looked perfect. Just like music videos, *Miami Vice* was all about appearance. The show's director, Lee Katkin, even admitted this to the press: "The show is written for an MTV audience, which is more interested in images, emotions, and energy than plot and character,"[8] he said. Katkin was right. The show was short on substance and long on style, and people loved it.

Miami Vice was just one example of how important music videos had become in the popular culture. This influence grew as the years passed. By the end of the 1980s musicians were the source of popular styles, slang, attitude, and more—thanks in large part to music videos.

Notes

Introduction: A Time of Change

1. Quoted in Nicolaus Mills, *Culture in an Age of Money: The Legacy of the 1980s in America*. Chicago: Elephant Paperbacks, 1990. http://eightiesclub.tripod.com.

Chapter One: The Cold War Ends

2. Quoted in Jeremy Isaacs and Taylor Downing, *Cold War: An Illustrated History, 1945–1991*. Boston: Little, Brown, 1998, p. 342.
3. The Reagan Information Page, "Great Quotes from President Reagan." www.presidentreagan.info.
4. Quoted in Isaacs and Downing, *Cold War*, p. 356.
5. Quoted in Isaacs and Downing, *Cold War*, p. 356.

Chapter Two: The Computer Revolution

6. Otto Friedrich, "The Computer Moves In," *Time*, Jan. 3, 1983, Infotrac. infotrac.galegroup.com.

Chapter Three: AIDS Appears

7. Quoted in William I. Johnston, *HIV-Negative: How the Uninfected Are Affected by AIDS*. New York: Insight Books-Plenum, 1995. world.std.com/~wij.

Chapter Four: Music Videos Change Society

8. Quoted in Jason Manning, "MTV, Madonna and Miami Vice," The Eighties Club. http://eightiesclub.tripod.com.

Glossary

AIDS: Acquired Immunodeficiency Syndrome. AIDS is a disease that weakens the immune system.

arms race: A competition between countries to develop more and bigger weapons.

communism: A social ideal that says all people should give according to their ability and take according to their needs.

epidemic: A large-scale outbreak of a disease.

floppy disk: A flexible storage card that records and stores computer files.

HIV: Human Immunodeficiency Virus. HIV is the virus that causes AIDS.

immune system: A bodily system that kills harmful germs.

productivity: The amount of work a person or group of people can do in a certain amount of time.

software: Programs that are designed to be run by computers.

spreadsheet: A computer program designed for record-keeping tasks, especially accounting.

superpower: An extremely dominant nation; one that controls and influences many other nations.

virus: A disease-causing microorganism.

word processor: A computer program that helps users with writing-related tasks.

For Further Exploration

Books

Margaret O. Hyde with Elizabeth Forsyth, *Know About AIDS*. New York: Walker, 1990. Examines many aspects of the AIDS epidemic, including its history, causes, the search for a cure, and more.

Nigel Kelly, *The Fall of the Berlin Wall: The Cold War Ends*. Chicago: Heinemann Library, 2001. Read about the event that many historians feel marked the end of the Cold War.

Scott Nance, *Music You Can See: The MTV Story*. Las Vegas: Pioneer, 1993. This book tells the story of MTV's rise.

Steve Parker, *Computers*. Austin, TX: Raintree Steck-Vaughn, 1997. An easy-to-understand overview of computers, including their history, construction, and uses.

Websites

The Eighties Club (http://eightiesclub.tripod.com). This website includes a wealth of information about every aspect of the 1980s.

The '80s Server (www.80s.com). Listen to the music of the 1980s, play games of the era, and much more.

Index

Picture Credits

Cover image: © CORBIS
AP/Wide World Photos, 40
© David Baauchli/Reuters/Landov, 14
© Bettmann/CORBIS, 28, 32
© CORBIS, 37, 39
© Deborah Feingold/CORBIS, 17
© Michael Freeman/CORBIS, 29
© Hulton/Archive by Getty Images, 35
Chris Jouan, 7
© Lawrence Livermore National Library/Photo
   Researchers, Inc., 12
© Alon Reininger/Contact Press Images/PictureQuest, 26
© Roger Ressmeyer/CORBIS, 18, 20, 23, 31
Courtesy of the Ronald Reagan Library, 11
© Bob Rowen; Progressive Image/CORBIS, 22
© Royalty-Free/CORBIS, 21
© Leif Skoogfors/CORBIS, 10

About the Author

Kris Hirschmann has written more than ninety books for children. She is the president of The Wordshop, a business that provides a wide variety of writing and editorial services. She holds a bachelor's degree in psychology from Dartmouth College in Hanover, New Hampshire.

Hirschmann lives just outside Orlando, Florida, with her husband, Michael, and her daughter, Nikki.